Top Notch Couples

The First 5 Skills

Author: Don Boice

Editor: Marian Sandmaier

Copyright C 2010 by Boice Counseling Publications

Written permission is required to reproduce, in any manner, in whole or in part, the material contained herein. Submit requests to:

donboice@boicecounseling.com

For the latest on books and relationships that will help your relationship, visit us online at:

www.boicecounseling.com

Contents

Introduction 5

Common Questions about Skill-Building 7

Relationship Skills Assessment 11

Skill 1: Communicating Fully 15

    Getting Started 16

    Men, Try This 17

    Common Errors 19

    "I" Statements 21

    Check for Understanding 23

Skill 2: Building Passion 25

    Exercise 1: Make a Gratitude List 27

    Exercise 2: Make a Passion List 30

    Exercise 3: Sharing the Spark 31

    Exercise 4: How Do You Promote Passion? 32

    Exercise 5: Score Points the Positive Way 35

    Exercise 6: The Language of Love 38

    Exercise 7: Take a Good Look 39

    Exercise 8: Picture Your Relationship 40

    Exercise 9: Love Shower 41

    Exercise 10: Name Your Passion Killers 42

    Check for Understanding 43

Skill 3: Making Time for Your Spouse 45

    Common Error 46

    Free Dates 47

    Low-Cost Dates 48

    How Busy Are You? 49

    Common Error 51

    Check for Understanding 51

Skill 4: Conversing with Ease 53

    Communicating Your Enthusiasm 55

    Common Errors 57

    Check for Understanding 58

Skill 5: Communicating Well with the Opposite Sex 61

    Examples of using this skill correctly 62

    Generalizations about Women's Communication Style 64

    Generalizations about Men's Communication Style 76

    General Common Errors in the Gender Discussion 83

    Check for Understanding 85

Conclusion 86

Workbook Feedback 87

Boice Counseling Publications 89

Introduction

The skills in this workbook are designed to help you develop a stronger relationship. If you and your partner learn the skills, practice them and use them appropriately, you will be less dependent on a therapist. You will be able to develop a healthier, more rewarding relationship on your own. That is the goal of therapy and the goal of this workbook. Once you learn, practice and master these skills, they will become yours.

Save yourself the cost of the first five counseling sessions, *if* you end up needing counseling.

The skills I have chosen are the ones most frequently requested by couples in early counseling. They are also the skills that, when *not* used, tend to worsen conflict in a partnership. If you master these skills and use them regularly, your relationship is likely to improve dramatically. The more skills you master and use, the more you will benefit. It just depends on what level of relationship you seek--good enough, great or Top Notch.

Note: I use "partner" and "spouse" interchangeably in this book to reinforce that successful relationships are about partnership. Additionally, you do not need to be married to benefit from this workbook, although I am writing this from the perspective of married couples.

When you start practicing these skills, they may feel awkward at first. In fact, you already know many of these skills, even if you have not yet mastered them. They aren't new to you. Once you have mastered them, they will feel natural and normal.

I wish for you a strong relationship, one that is fulfilling and helps you to reach your full potential.

All the best,

Don

Common Questions about Skill-Building

How will I achieve the goals in this workbook?

Practice each skill, evaluate yourself, and practice again. Have someone else tell you if they think you "get it."

Here are some more specific steps: Read each skill, and then practice it in the mirror. Then, either video yourself doing it and watch the video and give yourself feedback, or role-play with someone else and ask for feedback. Gradually, you will reach a level of comfort. Continue practicing after you have received feedback. By the time you receive additional feedback the second time through, you will approach mastery.

Why did you choose the particular skills described in this workbook?

The relationship issues raised in this workbook come out of my work with couples. The skills are those that couples come into counseling wanting to improve. They know that if they can improve these skills, their relationship will change. They may still disagree and experience conflict, but the arguing will be more dignified and the fights will be shorter in duration. Partners will respect one another more afterward. I tend to be very practical. I suggest that you try this approach. If it works for you and your partner, keep doing it. If it does not, I urge you to try something else.

Does a skills approach work?

Yes. Many couples simply lack relationship skills or forget to use the skills they have. When we focus on a skills approach, the assumption is that anyone can learn them and with practice, master them. The skills do not change who you are as a person. The skills simply improve your chances of communicating effectively. Improved communication will help you work through the vast majority of problems you face as a couple.

Let me be clear, though, that having and using skills won't necessarily save your marriage. Some problems cannot be solved. Some problems are not solved simply by improved communication. For example, if one partner in the couple has an affair and the couple responds by practicing these skills, they will now know how to communicate clearly and argue better. Communication alone will not solve this problem. The same is true with mental illness, addiction, and domestic violence. For these kinds of problems, I suggest that you work with a good therapist as well as this workbook.

Relationship Skills Assessment

Rate the skills you already have as Very Skilled (VS), Okay but not Great (O), Needs Work (NW) Write the code on the line preceding each statement:

- ☐ I can identify and express 10 feelings.
- ☐ I can express each of those feelings with my face and with other non-verbal communication.
- ☐ I can identify when I am about to get angry.
- ☐ I can stop myself from talking when I find myself getting angry.
- ☐ I regularly stop myself from saying mean things.
- ☐ I know how to repair the relationship when I have said/done mean things.
- ☐ I know how to communicate using "I" statements.
- ☐ I regularly actively listen, without interrupting.
- ☐ I regularly paraphrase what my partner has said.
- ☐ I regularly validate what my partner has said.
- ☐ I regularly catch myself when I feel myself becoming defensive.
- ☐ I regularly assert myself and my rights.

- ❑ I am able to set up a time to go out with my partner, get a babysitter, if needed, and arrange a place to go and how to get there, in a way that my partner appreciates.

- ❑ I am able to be spontaneous, drop everything and have fun.

- ❑ I know how to build passion for my partner.

- ❑ When feelings get really strong, I remain able to listen to my partner.*

- ❑ I can choose to not take personally what is being said to me.

- ❑ I express resentments when they come up, rather than hold them in.

- ❑ I express my conflicts and upsets with my partner with respect.

- ❑ I can identify and understand the effects of my childhood on my adult relationship choices and behaviors.

- ❑ I know many methods for forgiveness.

- ❑ I share my vision of this relationship with my partner.

- ❑ I express my love and appreciation in ways that my partner wants.

- ❑ I can create the right conditions for enjoyable conversation.

- ❑ I explore challenging subjects.

- ❏ I use conversation to get to know my partner and bring back interest.

- ❏ I am curious about my partner.

- ❏ I can disagree without nasty arguments.

Now, look again at the statements and focus specifically on the skills you need to work on. There are many skills involved in making a relationship work. Some are more important at different stages of a relationship.

Skill 1: Communicating Fully

Full communication means verbal (the words you use) and non-verbal (rolling eyes, crossing arms, slouching, using a flat tone of voice, etc.)

Often we use our words and forget to match our nonverbal behaviors to the words. When we forget to match, others have a hard time knowing what to believe. For example, imagine someone saying they won the lottery. They say it in a dull, bored voice. That doesn't match. It is not congruent with the words. The same thing holds true for saying, "I love you" in an aloof voice and without looking at the person.

Simply put, communication is not believable when the words do not match the nonverbal behavior. You therefore have incomplete communication or even mixed messages. When you can fully communicate, you have a much better chance of connecting and getting your point across. By the way, this works in the world of work as well as at home. Watch how the people with the best relationship skills tend to advance quickly. They make it easy for others to do business with them.

Getting Started

Practice expressing yourself fully.

Make a list of feelings.

Now, make a list of feelings you rarely express.

> **Note:** There are always some feelings that some people don't feel comfortable expressing.

If you need help, you can get a feelings list on the Internet or you can brainstorm different situations and how you might feel in each of them. Examples: Mad, sad, glad, happy, angry, distressed, lonely, guilty, afraid, irritated, annoyed, disenchanted, discouraged, disillusioned, loving, thrilled, and joyful.

For each feeling, try to remember the last time you felt that way.

Identify how intense the feeling was and where you felt it in your body.

Name the feeling out loud and ask yourself these questions.

- What tone of voice are you using as you say the word?

- Does your tone match the intensity of the word you are using?

- What are you communicating using your eyes, hands, shoulders, face and the volume of your speaking voice?

If you can, practice this at home in front of the mirror or even better, with a video camera. After you have practiced for a while, video yourself again. Contrast the before and after videos.

Men, Try This

Tell your wife or girlfriend, "When you/we _____, I feel _____."

Example

"When we spend time together, I feel really happy."

Say with proper inflection of voice and a smile on your face.

Be sure to practice this one, men. You already know this skill; it's just a little rusty. It is a variation of the way you talked with your partner when you first were courting.

Remember how romantic you were? Remember all the nice things you said to her? Back then, it seemed to just flow. Well, now you may have to work at it. Believe me; it will be worth the effort.

Why you might need this skill

As we discussed earlier, you cannot overcome every problem with better communication. But you can eliminate some useless arguments and you can connect better with your spouse. Also practice the skill at work and with friends. People will begin to relate to you differently as you communicate more effectively. Extra incentive: Some people have reported that after practicing this skill regularly on the job, they got a raise!

Common Errors

Many people, especially men, tend to focus more on thoughts than emotions. They might say, "I feel that you should not do that."

Notice that the word "feel" was there and yet no feeling was demonstrated. They were telling you what they *thought*, not directly what they felt.

A listener might be able to guess correctly how the speaker felt, but the onus is on the speaker to eliminate guesswork. Tell us how you felt.

Some men hold the whole "feeling world" in contempt. They do not see why they should have to re-learn this vocabulary, and they resent it. Some men refuse to participate in couples counseling with the excuse that they can't tolerate "all the touchy-feely." Really, what they are indicating is that they do not value full communication. If they did value it, they would change their style.

Other men offer the excuse that expressing their feelings more directly would change their personality, as if communication style was the same thing as personality. In fact, it is very different. For example, would you talk to a one-year-old the same way you would talk to an adult? Of course you wouldn't. You would change your style of communication, while remaining exactly who you are.

What might stop you from practicing this exercise correctly?

- Not knowing your feelings.
- Not wanting your spouse to know how you feel because you are feeling vulnerable or weak.

Add your own reasons below:

_____

_____

_____

_____

_____

Remember: If you practice this skill, you will begin to own it. Just reading it will not be enough. Picture your favorite athlete or musician and imagine how many times they had to practice their particular skills to master them. This is about commitment. You say you want to be a better communicator. Here is your chance to prove it.

"I" Statements

"I" statements are very simple and powerful, yet underused. They can be very useful in getting through the language barrier between men and women. They are especially helpful when you discuss something you know is going to be delicate.

Some examples of "I" statements

- I feel sad when you say that I don't love you.
- I feel angry when you call me names.
- I feel hopeful when I hear you are getting counseling for your anger.
- I feel scared when you say we might divorce.

- I feel disappointment when you say we're going out then you change your mind because you're too tired.

The key to effective "I" statements is that after using the word "feel," you must name an actual *emotion*. A lot of people tell us what they *think* rather than what they *feel*.

Examples of what you may feel

Agitated, frustrated, enraged, furious, silly, playful, rejected, abandoned, terrified, nervous, and concerned. Although using "I statements" may look simple, this skill is not always easy to carry out. Many of us are in the habit of starting difficult conversations with "*You* always…" Instead, start with, "I feel _____ when you _____."

So you'll need to practice starting with "I" on a regular basis. Then, when you find yourself in the midst of an emotion-charged situation, you'll stand a better chance of keeping things calm and honest with an effective "I" statement.

Check for Understanding

Answer the following questions.

- How does using an "I" statement improve communication?

- How do "I" statements help to break through the communications gender barrier?

- Full communication requires matching nonverbal behaviors with words. Given this reality, what might you infer about your current communications skills?

- What might happen in your marriage if you more closely matched your statements with your nonverbal behaviors?

Listen to the very next love song you hear. Listen closely to the words. Does the musician sing them in a heartfelt way, or does she/he just repeat the words? In other words, does he/she match the nonverbal to the verbal?

You can do the same with poetry. Try reading a love poem without changing the expression on your face (and without laughing!). Picture yourself doing this in front of your partner and imagine his/her expression.

What would it look like if you expressed the feelings in the poem without words? Go ahead and mime the feeling. When you are without words, the rest of your body needs to communicate better. Try this from time to time.

Please remember to practice this. It might be difficult at first; with practice it becomes easier and more natural. It is awfully important and sets the tone for your marriage. So, if you read it and did not practice, now is the time. Your relationship is worth it!

Skill 2: Building Passion

Please note that passion means more than just sexual passion.

There are times in every relationship when passion wanes. This is normal and natural. People fall in love and out of love and then in love and then out of love. The goal is to continue falling back in love with, and building passion for, the one with whom you are committed.

Many people simply give up when passion diminishes, as if a feeling is more important than the commitment they have made. Some people base a relationship on romance rather than love and commitment. But romance and sizzling-hot sexual attraction are obviously too fleeting to use as a basis for a long-term, intimate relationship.

This doesn't mean that passion isn't important. Research shows that for a marriage to work well, passion has to be at an acceptable level. To accomplish this, you have to build enough good feelings and reduce the amount of bad feelings. Otherwise, one spouse or the other will opt out.

The psychologist John Gottman, Ph. D. has estimated this ratio to be 5 good interactions to one bad interaction. If you can establish this ratio, your marriage is on the right track.

For more on Gottman's research and on how to boost your own "love ratio," I recommend any of his books. I share many of the same conclusions with him after years of doing my own anecdotal research. He has the empirical studies to show that what we already know to do, works well. He also has many ideas that are ahead of their time and many therapists have been greatly influenced by his work. I am one of those therapists.

Generally speaking, when you look for the positive, you find it. When you look for the negative, you find it. Which one do you want to look for?

Exercise 1: Make a Gratitude List

I am grateful for _____

Write down five of these a day and watch how your symptoms of anxiety and depression diminish. When you feel gratitude, you set yourself up for finding more positive in life. As you find more positive, many people experience a surge of passion about their daily life.

You can be grateful for anything in your life. Start with the basics: Being able to read, having enough money and resources to be learning this material, having a job, living indoors year round, having enough food, sleeping on a bed, having a pillow, having warm clothing in the winter — all are things to be grateful for.

When we take these things for granted, we are teaching ourselves to want and grasp more and more. This is guaranteed to bring us misery. When we are grateful for what we have, we remember what is important.

Besides, have you noticed that when you are appreciative and grateful, you simply feel better?

Now, think about your partner. What about him or her makes you feel grateful? Your partner must add something to your life (or have added something to your life in the past) or you would not have chosen to be with him or her.

Make a list of what you appreciate about your partner:

1

2

3

4

5

Add those to your daily gratitude list.

Locate Your Fire

In both my clinical and personal experience, a key to re-establishing marital passion is to find things about which you *yourself* feel enthusiasm. Look for them. (For example, I feel passion about soccer, helping couples keep their relationship together, and SCUBA Diving.) When you have passion and you look for it in your spouse, you are more apt to find it. If you lack passion in your daily life, your task is to find some!

Exercise 2: Make a Passion List

Naming your enthusiasms can help you to become more aware of them. Fill in the blanks below. I feel passionate about....

1

2

3

4

5

Becoming aware of your own passions is important. If I cannot get my own passion going, then I am not going to have passion for my wife. It makes sense: You are responsible for your own feelings, just as she is responsible for hers. This is our job as adults. When we make other people responsible for our own feelings, we feel like victims. When we own our own feelings, we become powerful.

Exercise 3: Sharing the Spark

Now, share with your spouse what she/he does that helps you light that spark. While you are still responsible for your own passion, your spouse can help you to engender it by his/her behaviors. Think about the time you spent with your partner when you were first dating. Look at pictures of your courtship. What do you notice?

- Were you doing activities you or your partner enjoyed? Were you having fun?
- Were you being of service to your partner?
- Were you being sexual?
- Were you rubbing each other's backs or providing other kinds of non-sexual comfort?
- Were you telling him or her how much you liked or loved him or her?
- Were you buying him or her little gifts or going out to dinner?
- What do you think might happen if you tried a few of these things now?

Exercise 4: How Do You Promote Passion?

Now, list several things that you do to bring passion into your relationship. Ask your partner to do the same.

Examples

- I plan dates for us and take care of all the details.
- I make a special meal for him or her.
- I go to couples yoga with my wife.
- I talk about what I like sexually and ask him or her the same.
- I ask her about her day and pay attention to her response.
- I call him at work.
- I write notes to her.
- I buy clothes I know he would like.
- I give her back rubs a couple times a week.
- I read him poetry.

- I ask her to dance with me.

- I tell him how manly he is.

- I tell her how beautiful she is.

- I regularly compliment him/her in other ways.

How might telling your spouse what you do to bring passion, actually help to bring passion into the relationship?

Now trade your lists. Look through them. Check for any surprises. Make sure you clarify that you really understand them. If there is one that you are unlikely to do, you may want to talk about that at some later point. The ones you find easy to do, you want to make sure that you fully understand and start planning when to do them. If your partner likes to be surprised, then make it a surprise. Just make sure that you use them and put them where you can easily access them.

Common Errors

If you think that passion is the basis for an adult, healthy relationship. Kids in high school think that way, and our whole society reinforces the notion that we should always feel "in love." That is simply wrong-headed. Over time, it is natural for passion to diminish.

Thinking that passion will come back if we keep doing what we're doing and don't talk about it. Instead, bring up the subject with your partner. Tell her, "I'd like to talk about the passion in our relationship." Or ask her, "How important is this to you?"

Exercise 5: Score Points the Positive Way

My wife and I made a list of things we liked and shared them with one another. I listed what I like to receive from her and how many points each "gift" was worth. 100 was the highest and 1 was the lowest. Getting her flowers from the grocery store was almost 50 and making sure the kitchen was spotless was about 5 points. She did the same for herself. It turned out that I had not been reading her mind very well, nor had she been reading mine. Once we found out what the other actually liked, it increased the odds that the other would do something positive and thereby "score points."

For example, I wrote: "She scores points with me when she <u>makes my lunch for me</u> (27 points)"

My wife wrote: "He scores points with me when he <u>Brings me those nice red carnations from the grocery store and puts them in a vase on the kitchen table</u> (45 points)"

Common Errors

You do not tally up points like in a sport. This is not a competition! The points are there for reference only, so that each of you knows what makes the other feel really, really good.

If you are keeping score and telling your spouse that you are 100 points ahead, you have misunderstood the idea. The idea is to score points without expecting anything in return. Expectations are key in relationships. If you expect everything you do to be acknowledged and appreciated and rewarded, you are highly likely to be disappointed. If you are keeping score, you are playing a power game.

Do you want him/her to be happy? Then score the points and do what you can to influence your partner's happiness. Do it without expectation of reward and you actually earn more points. (By the way, doing for others without expecting a reward is one of the secrets to happiness, too.)

If you consistently earn points on behalf of your spouse but your spouse rarely or never earns points for you, you do need to have a discussion. It could be as simple as, "I noticed that I've been doing a lot of the things on your points list for the past month or so. It seems like you have not been doing the ones on mine. Am I reading that correctly? Is everything okay between us?"

Exercise 6: The Language of Love

Ask for what you want from your partner. Do you like getting love notes or poems? Ask. Do you prefer holding hands or a back rub? Ask.

A love language is a way that someone more fully understands that you love them. Many men describe it this way, "I understand you love me when you speak the language of physical affection. You may still love me if you are not physically affectionate, but I understand it clearly if it is physical."

If you know your partner's "love language," you will have a better chance of helping the passion come back. For example, if my wife likes when I do little things for her and does not care if I write her notes, I will do little things for her. If I like when she rubs my back, but she writes me love notes, that does not quite do it for me.

For more on that read <u>Languages of Love</u> - a great book! You will have to reach her in *her* love language, so that she understands that you love her.

Exercise 7: Take a Good Look

Gaze into each other's eyes for 5 minutes. Gaze without staring each other down or giggling too much. Look into your partner's pupils as deeply as you can. Now, try doing it while holding hands. How do you feel when you connect on this level? Is this something that you would like to repeat with your partner? There are many ways of connecting. Please keep looking until you find a way that works for you and your partner.

Exercise 8: Picture Your Relationship

Create a timeline, with photos, of your dating and first 10 years of marriage. Continue in 10-year increments. Put it up on the wall and just be in awe of all that you have shared. Look at all you have been through together. Look at all the memories you have created together.

You might also look at home movies together. It's another opportunity to experience how much shared history you have. Think about the positive things—especially people and experiences—that your spouse has helped to bring into your life.

Exercise 9: Love Shower

Person 1 volunteers to hear Person 2 say wonderful things about Person 1. Spend a few minutes on this one; don't rush it. Then switch: Now Person 1 does the "love showering" and Person 2 is the recipient.

For example, "I love that you read books on how to improve our relationship. I feel closer to you when you do that." Or "I really like how you keep our family together. You reach out to my parents and invite them for Holiday dinners."

Exercise 10: Name Your Passion Killers

Just as there are things we can do to promote passion, there are things we can do to strangle it. List the things you do to kill passion in your relationship. Ask your partner to do the same. (We can't change them until we name them.) They can be things you do on purpose or just by accident.

Examples

- I work too much
- I don't tell her that I love her
- I can be really selfish
- I don't help out around the house
- I nag too much
- I don't make time for him
- I invalidate her feelings
- I don't listen
- I try to fix the problem instead of just listening
- I am too critical
- I expect too much

Add your own Passion Killers

-
-
-
-

Check for Understanding

- What might happen if we moved beyond our need to be perpetually "in love" and instead based our relationships on friendship?

- What does your logic say about how long that type of hot, ultra-romantic relationship is likely to last?

- What might be the relationship of our desire to be "in love" to the national divorce rate?

Thank you for investing the time in your relationship. Please make sure that the information here becomes yours. Practice it until it becomes a habit or natural and your partner will appreciate how spontaneous you have become.

Skill 3: Making Time for Your Spouse

Not long ago, researchers did a study showing that having a regular date with your spouse is likely to improve your relationship.

Thank you researchers, we already knew that! Many time researchers will come up with a finding and lay claim to that knowledge when the rest of us have already been doing the same thing for years.

But knowing it isn't the same as doing it. The fact is, if you regularly date your spouse, you are more likely to stay married. If you do not, you are all but guaranteeing the demise of your relationship. You may not divorce, but you will not be happily married.

Making time for your spouse will help not only your marriage, but your children as well. A happy relationship is the best gift you can give your children. Show your children that your spouse comes first, even before the children. The worst thing you can do is confuse your child into thinking they come before your spouse. Your spouse is the primary relationship and if the marital relationship is solid, the needs of the children will be more likely to be met.

Ask yourself these questions

- Do we want to set up a "date night" or are we actively avoiding one another?
- How often do we go out, just the two of us?
- What do we talk about when we are out?
- How often do we talk about the relationship and work on our friendship?

Satisfied couples with children report dating as much as once a week. They set aside time and spend about 30 minutes talking. They tend to avoid things like movies because that reduces their interaction time. Interaction is the goal.

Common Error

Coming up with excuses. "There is not enough time or money." We all know these are lame excuses. There is *always* enough time and money to do what is most important to us. We show our priorities through how we spend time and money.

Free Dates

Does the date have to be free? Not necessarily. But think back to childhood and how often you enjoyed simple things that didn't cost a thing. Don't let a lack of money become an excuse. Brainstorm ways you could spend time with one another and not spend a dime, such as walking on the beach, talking on the back deck while drinking something from the fridge, while the kids are in bed upstairs. One woman suggested that her husband would be more up for this if there were sex involved sometime during the date. (She pointed out that sex is free.)

List all the free dates you can think of

1

2

3

4

5

6

Low-Cost Dates

How about making a calendar of two date nights a month that are under 10 dollars? You might make them "seasonal," such as going out for ice cream in the summer, taking a walk in the fall to see the leaves, going out for coffee in the winter, riding bikes in the spring, throwing in something with sports for the sports lover each season. Date nights can be a great way to earn points.

Example: If I go to a yoga class with my wife, I would win tons of points. If she went to a jazz concert with me, she would win tons of points.

Make a list of low-cost dates

1

2

3

4

5

6

How Busy Are You?

Everybody's busy. But let's examine just *how* busy you are.

Are we talking you don't have an hour a week? Seriously? Not even an hour? Not even after the kids go to bed?

If not, are they going to bed at a reasonable time?

Are you somehow setting up the kids to come between the two of you? (Example: The kids sleep in the bed with the husband and wife. This defines the adults only as parents, not as husband and wife in their own marital bed.) I challenge you to put your marriage ahead of your children. A marriage needs about as much nurturing as children do, but we rarely give it that much.

Do you have an hour a week to check e-mail, watch TV, read the paper etc.? Sorry, then I'm not buying the excuse that you do not have enough time.

Have you structured your life in such a way that you rarely see one another? If so, please realize you are choosing to neglect your marriage. You have chosen something else as more important than your relationship.

Is something else going on where you've simply agreed to live together and not address the issues that stare you in the face?

Don't make the mistake of thinking "Oh, I already know my spouse. There's no need to spend special time together." The fact is, people who are on a path of growing continue to change. As soon as you think you know your spouse, he or she has begun to change and you have to get to know him or her all over again. If you are both lucky, this process of growing and changing—and getting to know each other again—will continue for the rest of your lives.

Common Error

Some people mistakenly believe that simply being in the same room qualifies as "quality time." This is not what we mean here. Quality time is time spent getting to know one another. It includes talking about what matters. Really getting to know each other has its risks, but also the potential for deep rewards for your relationship.

Check for Understanding

Answer the following questions.

- What is the relationship between regular "date nights" and being happily married?

- How would you categorize your current dating style as compared to when you were first dating your spouse?

- How do you think regular dating would affect your children's sense of security and happiness?

- What might you conclude from the excuses you and your spouse make about dating?

- What might happen if you overcame all of the obstacles and had time to get to know one another regularly?

- Are you honestly willing to go on dates?

Visualize you and your spouse going out on a regular basis, each one of you planning 50 percent of the dates and having smiles on your faces, going places where you are happy and having shared experiences about which to talk. When you visualize this, how do you feel?

While I think this is good information, it is more valuable when you practice it and reinforce the habit. Do this regularly. It is a bit of a stretch when time feels tight. You can do it!

Skill 4: Conversing with Ease

Many people would like to have spicy, interesting conversations with their partner, but they don't know how to initiate and maintain such a conversation. How do you get started?

Most of us have some area of passion, interest or excitement in our lives. If you talk about what you are interested in, your passion will show through and ignite the conversation. If you share your excitement, your partner will be more likely to share hers/his.

- What are you excited about now? (both personally and professionally)
- What is happening in your life right now? (people, activities, books, movies—anything!)
- What are a few of the most important events in your life?
- Who have been some of the most important people in your life?
- What is your vision for the future?

Any of these subjects can start a good conversation. The key is to both convey your own thoughts AND **ask** the other person for their input.

Example

- I am reading this great book about people who get easily overstimulated. Yeah, they walk into a store and really shut down. They can't turn off the stimuli. I think I do that sometimes. Do you ever have that happen?

- I keep thinking about all these water conferences and how there could be a war over water. We live in the Great Lakes Region and near the Finger Lakes. Do you suppose we will be impacted by any water shortages?

- If you could do it all over again, what sports would you like to play?

- If you won the lottery, what would you do differently?

- Sometimes I look at how tough life can be. We are so busy at work, with the kids, running around everywhere. I feel like I don't have my own life some days. Did you ever think life would be this way?

All of these "openers" are invitations to get to know one another and find out more about each other's interests, priorities, feelings and thoughts. Try some of them out on your partner. Practice this skill every day.

Communicating Your Enthusiasm

Verbally

- What words do you use to convey that you really care about a topic?
- What words to you use to encourage your spouse to join the conversation and/or continue talking about the topic?

Nonverbally

- Do your words match your tone of voice and your body posture?

    For example, to maintain a conversation, you might say, "Uh huh, go on, tell me more" and also turn your body toward the person. This shows that you are listening, focusing just on them.

- Do you say you are interested, yet keep the laptop or TV on in front of you?

    What else might you do to give "mixed messages" to your partner about your level of interest in the conversation?

- How do you show via nonverbal messages that you're enthusiastic about what your partner is talking about?

    If you are not enthusiastic about the conversation, what kind of language might you use to tactfully communicate that?

Common Errors

When you feel bored in the relationship, <u>ask yourself if you are contributing to the boredom.</u> If you take responsibility for your feelings on this, you will find it easier to escape boredom. Why? You are responsible for how you feel. If you are bored, you are responsible for creating that feeling. If you blame 100% of your boredom on your spouse, you are interpreting the situation incorrectly. You are responsible for how you feel.

Some people make excuses for not developing conversational skills, such as, "I'm not a big talker-- that is just not who I am." The mistake there is failing to realize that your communication style is changeable. You may not be able to change your personality, but you can change your *style*.

Think about it this way: Do you communicate with a two-year-old the same way you do with your co-workers?

Check for Understanding

Ask yourself these questions:

- Are your current conversations with your spouse very different than the ones you had when you were first dating? How so?

- Do you see a relationship between initiating a conversation and being interesting and getting rid of boredom?

- How might starting an effective conversation be different at home than it might be at work?

- What is interesting to you?

- What might happen if you stopped maintaining a particular conversation with your spouse? How might he/she feel?

- What would happen if your spouse stopped maintaining a conversation with you? How would you feel?

- What alternatives should be considered if you find yourself struggling to maintain a conversation?

Think of a song or poem you have heard that speaks to this topic. Consider writing a song or poem that relates to this topic.

How would you describe your own ability to keep a conversation going? What steps might you take to improve your ability?

In closing, most couples complain about communication. Communication style is not the same as personality. You can change how you communicate and have wonderful impact on those around you. Thank you for taking the time to practice and rehearse this. It is time well spent!

Skill 5: Communicating Well with the Opposite Sex

Have you noticed that men and women communicate very differently? To be more specific, there are masculine ways of communication and feminine ways of communication. Not all women communicate using the feminine style and not all men use the masculine style. We are different, not better. You are different, not better. Consider it to be like different languages. Can you imagine saying that one language is better than another language? What needs to happen is that both styles need to understand and be able to communicate in both. What tends to happen is that in some couples, one partner refuses to speak the other person's language, making one person do all the work.

If we go blindly into female-male communication, we run the risk of communicating poorly and possibly even offending one another. Have you ever said something to someone of the other gender and found that she/he thought they understood what you meant, but actually didn't? Then this topic is for you.

Examples of using this skill correctly

- I think we just miscommunicated. Can I check this out with you?

- Let's try some "I" statements. I know those tend to break through gender barriers.

- I was trying to say _____. What did you hear me say?

- Tell me more about your problems at work today. It sounds awful.

- How would you like me to be supportive of you? Would you like me to just listen, or would you like me to problem solve with you?

- Then what happened?

Memorize the statements above and use them often to get through gender communication difficulty.

One of the best books on this topic is Deborah Tannen's *You Just Don't Understand.* Following are some key ideas from her book, confirmed by men and women with whom I have worked. We all owe her a debt of gratitude for her work on this. Please read the book, it is excellent!

Let's start with some generalizations about each gender. Do you recognize any of these characteristics in yourself? In your spouse?

Generalizations about Women's Communication Style

Women - 1

Women tend to appreciate relationships differently than men do. They want to feel connected and most of the communication is seen through the lens of connection. Therefore, they want to hear how you feel (your emotions, not your thoughts) and that they are not alone. They want to know if you have felt the same way or if something similar has happened to you. This is called "relating." If you can relate to what they are saying, they feel a sense of connection. Even if the feeling is one of the ones many guys don't like to talk about, they will feel closer to you if you try to relate. If you want to connect with a woman in your life, consider looking at your behavior and your language through her lens of connection. I have heard women say, "I would walk through the fires of Hades for a man who will understand me and connect with me."

Are you expressing feeling and are you giving them the sense that they are not alone? Are you connecting? What do you need to change, right now?

Common Errors

- Some men think that anything to do with feelings is below them. This is called contempt. Another way to explain it is that they feel superior to people who express emotions. Feeling superior to someone is not an effective way to connect. If you do not care about connecting with her and she cares about connecting with you, there is a larger problem.

- In mixed settings, <u>men tend to dominate the conversation</u> by talking, holding the floor and changing the topic. This is not the same thing as connecting and most women will feel some variation of resentment when this happens.

- It would be an error for a woman to think that a man does not want to connect, simply because he does not do this the way that a woman might do it. Men connect differently than women connect. We are simply different, not right, not wrong, just different. Explain to your partner how you would like to connect.

Women - 2

As a way to deepen connection, women want understanding and sympathy for their emotions and the events of their lives. When they talk, they are looking for an emotional response from you, which indicates you understand what they were saying. This is what they call "support."

Common Error

- Men typically try to solve problems, which does not work when women simply need support. If a man hears a problem, he needs to think about who sent the message. When men get together, they solve problems and this is okay. When you have someone from each gender, this does not work. He thinks he is doing the right thing, helping. However, problem-solving can make women feel angry and resentful. It is as if he is telling her that she cannot solve her problem on her own. It would be a mistake to do problem solving with a woman unless she asks him to. It would be a mistake for a woman to think that a man is intending to insult her, when he is problem solving.

- Invalidating and telling her she should not feel a certain way does not deepen the connection. For example, "You shouldn't feel that way. You should be happy that I _____."

What to try instead

Try offering understanding and support. Express how you understand her (clarify what you think she is saying and make sure you really got it) and you are golden. Ask her if she is looking for support and listening or if she is looking for your help in solving the problem BEFORE you offer her your insights.

Women - 3

Women ask questions and prompt the person who is talking to continue. "Tell me about… How was…?" This keeps the conversation going for women and for men. If there is conversational flow, women feel connected and close to you. Notice how much emphasis is on listening, not talking.

Common Error

Men tend to not prompt the other person or encourage them to continue talking. They have valid reasons for doing this; however, this results in not feeling connected to men. Women put up with this, but it does not leave them with warm fuzzy feelings toward men.

It would be a mistake to think that men do not want the conversation to continue. Just as the woman is continuing the conversation in a feminine style, the man is continuing the conversation in a masculine style. Neither one is wrong for wanting to communicate in their dominant style. The difficulty is when it consistently happens and affects the relationship.

Bring in this insight and things can change more easily. By the way, men exchange information. They talk to give or get information, not connection. When each gender has a different motivation for communicating, there is bound to be some difficulty.

Women - 4

Women use eye contact to let you know they are engaged and listening. A woman might nod her head and say a couple words to prompt. Nodding her head does not mean she agrees. It means she is "back channeling"—encouraging the speaker to continue. It means, "Go on, I am listening."

Common Errors

- Some men misinterpret this gesture as agreement. Try eye contact with her when you are listening. You may be happily surprised by her response.

- Some people mistake eye contact with intimacy. If she is making eye contact, do not make assumptions, ask.

Women - 5

Women want details and stories to connect. They will likely ask more questions than you will.

Common Error

- Some men say this makes them feel like they're being interrogated or grilled. They are not grilling you. The intention is to show they care. More details equals more caring. Women are also likely to ask different questions than men will ask.

- When a woman asks, "How was your day?" and you answer, "Fine," she hears that you do not want to connect to her. She feels you are dismissing her. If you provide details and stories, that tells her that you want to be in relationship with her. It tells her that you value her.

Women - 6

Women tend to take emotions and relationships very seriously.

Common Errors

If you hold emotions in contempt, you are holding a woman's highest priorities in contempt. Emotions are the basic building blocks of connection. If you approach life from a logical standpoint and she approaches the world from emotions, you are both right. They each work for you. But if you persist in speaking your own language, only, you will threaten the relationship. Each of you needs to bend a little. If you both bend, the connection will be much stronger. She will know you care and are making an effort. Additionally, since she values relationships, when she sees that you are not taking care of your own relationships, she may worry about you and about you and her. If you are letting relationships go in your family, she may feel threatened by that.

Women - 7

Women often add tags after saying something. Example, "The political situation drives me a little crazy, ya know?" The tag "ya know" lightens the statement or makes it more tentative, allowing the other person some leeway.

Common Error

This does not mean she is wishy-washy or wimpy. She has been trained to value relationships over decisiveness. If she is tentative in her statements, it preserves the relationship better. She is recognizing that some relationships are fragile and she is not willing to rock the boat simply to be decisive.

Women - 8

Women tend to like to talk about personal things—problems in life, their families, their experience on the job. This is how women connect and bond.

Common Errors

- If you also talk about these things in your life and their life, you have a better chance of bonding with your partner. If you refuse, for whatever reason, you will miss out on the depth of the relationship.

- It would be a mistake to think that men who do not talk about personal things do not want to connect and bond. Men do connection and bonding differently than women do. Many men report not feeling closer at all after talking about those personal things and cannot understand why women think it would be a bonding experience.

Women - 9

Women tend to stand closer and use their hands when they're talking. Why not experiment with this with the woman in your life?

Common Error

Stepping back from her when she is standing close. She wants the closeness. It would be a mistake to think that stepping back is rejection. He may be stepping back to accommodate her. "She didn't realize she was in my space, so I stepped back," is what I have heard men say.

Women - 10

Women tend to respond quickly, which extends conversations.

Common Error

Sometimes, men are put off by quick responses. Some men report not thinking quickly, therefore, not responding quickly. They would rather not talk than feel dominated by the woman in their life, they say. But for women, this is a way of showing interest in you and in the conversation, which builds connection.

Try this

Keep thinking about her behavior and her lens of connection. A woman's behavior will almost always make sense to you if you see it from her perspective.

Generalizations about Men's Communication Style

Now let's turn to the way men tend to communicate. Women, read this to understand your partner better. Men, read this and you may recognize yourself!

Keep in mind that while men and women tend to communicate for different reasons and with different styles, neither side is wrong. Both are right—just different. They often affect the other gender in a consistent way.

Men - 1

Men tend to try to show how strong and powerful they are. They hold the floor longer and tend to talk about information rather than people. They tend to direct the subject of the conversation and then interrupt more.

Common Error

I have heard women respond to this with, "That's just dumb." That smacks of contempt, not understanding. Attempt to understand it. If you do not agree after you get it, that is one thing.

Remember: Dismissing it out of hand is as bad as when men dismiss what is important to you.

Consider this: Most males of any species do something to attract the female. If it did not work, we would have evolved out of it into something that did work. There are 6 billion people on the planet, so on some level this behavior works for our species.

Men - 2

Men tend to problem-solve, gathering facts and arriving at solutions. When men talk with other men, problem-solving is natural.

Common Error

When problem-solving happens in a male-female conversation, it often is a problem for her. Women, don't assume that the man is trying to run your life, control you or not listen. Problem-solving is his default mode. If you ask him not to do it, you are asking him to change his default mode. That may also be considered controlling by some people. If you bring a man a problem, make sure you tell him whether or not you are looking for a solution. That is a win-win. Let him know in advance what you want from him and allow him to please you.

Men - 3

Men tend to avoid discussing feelings or topics that are too personal. This would actually undermine their feeling of power, which they want to preserve.

Common Error

It would be a mistake to think that men are terribly lonely or unhappy because they communicate this way. To think that men are "doing it wrong." To think that this way of communicating is not valid. To think that they do not connect or want to connect. Remember, not all men do every masculine piece, just as not all women use just the feminine communication parts.

So what do men like to talk about? Any topic that helps them feel powerful, any topic about which they know a lot of information.

Men - 4

Men tend not to encourage the other to talk more. If the man encourages the other to talk more, he is conveying that she/he is more powerful than he is. That would be working at cross-purposes, from his standpoint.

Common Error

- It would be a mistake to think that men sit down before every conversation and consciously figure out how to feel powerful. The person who talks more, has more information, and interrupts generally has more power.

- Studies have shown that although the stereotype is that women talk more, it is only true in different circumstances. It strongly depends on the topic and the setting.

Men - 5

Men tend to respond slowly, which slows down conversations. Slowing down a conversation allows him to maintain his power position.

Common Error

It is not true that this is a conscious process for most men. Many men report not being able to think on their feet. Their wives tend to be much more verbal than they are. The only way they feel they can compete, is if the pace is slow enough to allow them to process their thoughts/feelings. If women allow the conversation to go too quickly, many men feel overwhelmed.

Men - 6

Men tend to have trouble expressing sympathy or understanding. Why would a man want to express sympathy? That puts him in the field of emotions. Many men do not feel competent when it comes to feelings.

Common Error

It would be wrong to think that the feelings do not exist. They exist below the surface and often remain unexpressed. Expressing feelings is often seen as a feminine thing. Most men avoid being seen as feminine, at all costs. As a man, being called feminine is not considered a compliment. If there is anything going wrong with power between partners, is he really going to express understanding and make himself vulnerable?

Men - 7

Men tend to talk more in public and less in private. Talking in public shows off his status. If he can reel off multiple facts and anecdotes, tell funny stories and jokes and otherwise hold the floor in public, he wins big points in the man world.

Common Error

- Assuming that he is going to be the same in public and in private. Many women complain that their man is not the same at home as he is at work or with friends. It would be unrealistic to expect him to be the exact same. If you like how he is in those other environments, consider having both of you together and add some friends or go out to dinner with some co-workers.

- That it is easy to always be on and perform, holding the floor.

General Common Errors in the Gender Discussion

Overgeneralizing

Of course, not *all* men behave this way and not *all* women behave that way. It's important not to cubbyhole either gender. But understanding the tendencies of each gender can be helpful in "getting" the other gender's conversational behavior. It helps us not take it personally or categorically think the others are doing it wrong.

Holding the other gender's preferred conversational style in contempt

Surveys shows that both men and women prefer to talk with women, as women do more work in most conversations. There are some things men can learn from women and women can learn from men. This is one of them.

Don't give up on meaningful conversation because your partner's style seems so different from yours. Instead, ask questions to find out more about what is going on. For example, you might say: "You don't seem to be encouraging me to talk today. Is everything all right?" or "You seem to be talking and then you stop when I begin talking about feelings. What is happening?"

I can't emphasize this enough: Keep checking in with each other! Assume that there are conversational style differences and regularly ask what your partner is trying to convey. Practice asking. Practice checking your assumptions. Recognize that there will be misunderstandings at times. That is the default. Don't get discouraged. With practice, both of you can grow and stretch toward the other's way of understanding the world.

Check for Understanding

Ask yourself these questions.

- How would you describe your own personal style of communication- all male, mostly male, all female, or mostly female?
- How well do you speak your partner's language?
- How does the male need for power and control lens affect your biggest fights?
- How does the female need for connection affect your biggest disagreements?
- Do you think you can truly know one another without knowing one another's language?
- What might happen if each of you cut the other some slack and began speaking the other's language as well as your own?
- Try to visualize what it would look like if you tried to stretch your own conversational style and meet your partner halfway.
- What songs can you think of that illustrate the gender differences in communication?

Conclusion

Look back to the skills listed at the beginning of the workbook. All of those skills will improve your relationship. The skills we just reviewed and worked through will start you on your way and you can build off them. If you master and use the skills in this workbook and no others, your relationship will improve.

If you would like to move your relationship closer to a top notch relationship, continue the process of building skills. Master the skills you have and then develop the next set. A mistake some couples make is to rush the process and have a set of skills that they know, but have not mastered. Stay tuned for more skills as we continue our work together in the next workbook.

I wish you all the best in your relationship. May your skills be strong and may you have the confidence that the two of you can handle anything together!

Workbook Feedback

It would be very helpful if you would take a few minutes to be honest and direct, as I am trying to improve the workbook. If you have feedback about something please e-mail me at donboice@boicecounseling.com

What would you have liked more of in the workbook?

What would you have liked less of in the workbook?

What skills would you have added or deleted?

If you had the option of downloading the workbook instead having a hard copy, would you like that?
____Yes ____No

Would you recommend this workbook to someone else? ____Yes ____No

Why or why not?

Boice Counseling Publications

Upcoming Topics from Boice Counseling Publications:

- Conflict and Anger Management DVD for Couples
- Couples Homework: What to do Between Sessions
- Choosing a Partner: How to Screen Better
- Are Men Always Wrong?
- Gender Communication: How to Understand What They Are Saying

To place your order, please visit
www.boicecounseling.com

Please note that Boice Counseling also offers Retreats for Couples, and Presentations to help people get along. Boice Counseling is a male-friendly counseling center. While it is friendly to women, like all counseling tends to be, it strives to make certain that men also feel comfortable.

Made in United States
North Haven, CT
31 May 2023